D0735598

Teeth Not Tears: Smiles Through the Rubble

Published by Shannon Enete through Createspace

ISBN-13: 978-1461046752

ISBN-10: 1461046750

Teeth Not Tears:

Smiles through
the rubble

Shannon Enete

Contents

Acknowledgements

To Thaylord and Wilbens, whose hearts have displayed a depth that has forever changed how I view life.

"Teeth Not Tears" would not have been possible without those whose generosity enabled my trip to Haiti: Denver and Susan Vold, Joe and Kirsten Rysko, Uncle Mac and Aunt Kim Parsons, Kayden and Jason Howard, Aaron Casady and Hugo Salido, Shane Enete, Greg and Anita Bergman, Brian and Julie Devader, Edith McCandless (Nana), John Arnett, Noel and Denise Enete, MedAct Employee Association, Penny McCaskill, and finally Thomas and Tina Loats.   Thank you from the bottom of my changed heart.

To my Editor-in-Chief and love of my life Leigh Rysko who has helped to make this book comprehensible and enjoyable to all. Additional thanks to Kayden Howard, for her edits and many improvements, and to Jill Hardy for all of her support and guidance.

Preface

As I wheeled my gurney back to the ambulance, a news report referencing the earthquake in Haiti caught my eye. I was working as a Paramedic providing care for citizens who call 9-1-1. Having spent my childhood near the San Andreas Fault, I was not initially concerned. Growing up, I used to jump onto my couch when we had an earthquake and pretend to surf while the ground shook. None of the earthquakes that I had experienced resulted in much damage.

Then images of Haiti began pouring in. I saw the overwhelming human need, pain, suffering, and gut-wrenching devastation. My heart sank. I silently reprimanded myself for my previous thoughts that undercut their immense loss. I, along with millions of people, became engrossed in news pertaining to Haiti. I felt a connection and a responsibility as a fellow human being to do something. I had disaster training and was compelled to help. It took over two months to secure all of the necessary coverage for work and finances to make it happen.

My plane landed safely in Port-au-Prince Haiti in early April, 2010. This was long after the bodies had been removed. In April, the sun was blaring and the cement cloud that once overpowered the city had been reduced to a smog-like presence. Haitians no longer coated their nares with toothpaste or wore facemasks. The streets expelled higher decibels than I could have imagined possible for such small roads. Busyness dominated the scene as people flooded the streets, strutting with purpose. Cars, motorbikes, and pedestrians weaved through every nook and cranny. Everyone headed in different directions coordinated with a common goal: survival.

It took days as a medical volunteer before my cognitive recognition of the devastation sank into a gut-felt response. The tragic tales I absorbed day after day twisted my insides. I had never exposed my eyes, ears, nose, and heart to circumstances so dire.

Ten days later, it was time for my departure. As I began to tear up, one of Heart to Heart's Haitian interpreters, Jean Fournes Thaylord, who goes by Thaylord, placed his hand on my shoulder. Wearing a huge, toothy grin, he said, "Teeth, not tears," a lesson I will take with me everywhere I go.

I will never fully understand the depth of angst and loss that my Haitian friends have been forced to endure. This book bears witness to the strength and beauty of the Haitian people through the Thaylord brothers' soulful eyes.

(Left) Wilbens Thaylord, (Right) Jean Fournes Thaylord

Teeth Not Tears depicts the Thaylords' lives in a true light to the best of my ability. The content was compiled through dozens of interviews with the brothers. The facts regarding Haiti are not academic; instead Wilbens and Thaylord have provided them. I did not validate each statement with "official" records, as my purpose is to portray their lives from their vantage. Their story is told in the first person, weaving from one brother's perspective to the other.

Popular Haitian proverbs complement their accounts throughout the book.

I authored Teeth Not Tears to raise awareness of the situation in Haiti, and to inspire the world with the Thaylords' demonstration of love and contentment.

Turning the Page

Haiti of the Past

The sun invaded my home through the window panes as I longingly peered out. The intensity of its warmth teased my skin. It wasn't enough. I longed to play outside, soaking myself in the sun, but the danger that existed far outweighed my toddler curiosity of the world.

I am no different than you. The only things that separate us are the cards that life has dealt. I was born in Port-au-Prince, Haiti, one of three boys. Growing up in Haiti in the 80's was night and day from the experience that the children of today are having. The town had a sleepy feel to it; citizens walked to a slower beat than that which is required today. I was treated to a blazing sun almost every day of the year. The streets were

1

clean and open.   The buildings in Port-au-Prince, sparse in number, exuded a French Colonial Style. Ocean views remained unobstructed. Things were difficult, and our government was self-serving, but even so, I sensed a clear cohesion as a people.

Every country has a personality. Haiti's personality was and still is smiley.   Smiles are proudly worn throughout the country even though some might wonder what we have to smile about. Haiti embodies resolve, strength, gratitude, and contentment.   We believe that complaining spurs weakness. So people rarely complain in Haiti. Instead, we fix what we don't like, or are at peace with that which we cannot change. I'm not sure when the Serenity Prayer was written, but I believe the author had Haitians in mind when he wrote it.

Teeth Not Tears

"God grant me the serenity
to accept the things I cannot change;
courage to change the things I can;
and wisdom to know the difference."

~Reinhold Niebuhr~

Basic needs were met through a variety of methods depending on what region of the island you called home. Those who lived near the ocean fished for much of their subsistence needs. Others farmed vegetables, sugar cane, coconuts, coffee, or bananas.

Energy was a major challenge. Rural Haiti did not have electricity. In order to cook, coal became a costly resource. Increased demands for coal caused widespread deforestation throughout the country. This in combination with political instability slowly reduced the capacity for agriculture to yield profit. Thousands of Haitians migrated to my town, the capital, in the hopes of a new job and new beginnings.

This ignited the era of clogged streets, overpopulation and staggering unemployment rates that we currently face. Back then, congestion wasn't part of our vocabulary.

Despite constant political upheavals, life was fairly simple as a Haitian boy. Families are very close in Haiti, even if geographic distance separates us. Family is all that we have, and all that we need. Boys were expected to play outside, free from responsibility or work until our later school years. Haitian girls unfortunately were not afforded the same experience. Instead they were required to help with house chores such as cooking, cleaning, and laundry as early as five years of age.

Port-au-Prince did have its benefits, like electricity twenty-four hours a day! Sunday nights used to be very special for young adults. It was what we looked forward to each week. We congregated at the local bar or club, drank a beer, and simply enjoyed ourselves. Nothing crazy or too exciting, and yet political changes in 1990-1991 halted the practice.

Haiti of Today

Today, chaotic encapsulates an average day in Haiti. People, cars, dogs, and motorcycles dart in and out of the small streets that serve Port-au-Prince. Citizens walk briskly with purpose; each route and vector is utilized, resulting in the highest yield of people accomplishing their various tasks.

Buildings are built one directly adjacent to another as if they were set up as dominos pieces. Streets are dirty, broken, and muddy at best. The main market is paved with trash that has become a permanent fixture to the area due to vehicles compressing layer upon layer so that it comprises the topcoat over dirt and rock.

With the traffic of today, I sometimes travel two inches in two hours. You would think from the volume of vehicles, that we all had our own vehicles but it is quite the opposite. Most of us use tap-taps to get around town.

A tap-tap is usually comprised of a small pickup with welded benches in the bed of the truck. It also sports some form of metal housing that provides relief from the sun for the passengers. The trucks are often decorated with bright murals that add an artistic flare to each vehicle. When one of the twenty or so passengers who cram into the truck needs to get off they simply tap on the truck twice signaling the driver to stop; hence the term tap-tap.

Crime has grown to be an enormous problem in a few areas in Port-au-Prince, so much so that the police refuse to enter the areas most teeming with violence. This leaves the ill at heart free to do whatever it is they desire without fear of consequence.

Roughly seventy-five percent of our schools were destroyed in the earthquake. Very few have even temporary reconstruction, which translates to numerous children missing out on a formal education. Some schools resumed classes outside due to lack of available safe infrastructure.

Children raised in tent camps are having a completely different experience than I did. Their home is often comprised of a bed sheet, a piece of sheet metal and whatever cardboard they can find to prop up against their neighbor's tent. The space is often four feet by three feet providing shelter for a family of four. The bed sheets aren't waterproof, and could blow away at any moment.

There are a few positive differences. Most tent camps have an NGO providing free medical care, something that most of the residents had never experienced prior to the earthquake. They also receive limited food vouchers from the World Food Bank and The Red Cross. I do not explain the situation in Haiti to complain, only to inform. Knowledge is the key to reform.

The Haiti of today has many new problems that need to be dealt with. Living in communes with no bath facilities, electricity, fresh water, or appropriate waste disposal system has lead to a bacteria heyday. The majority of Haitians contract scabies, skin rashes, worms, genital infections, STDs, and a variety of other infections.

Housebound

" When the power of love overcomes the

love of power, the world will know

peace." Jimi Hendrix

The history of my country is saturated with greed, corruption, military coups d'état, and violence. It is important, however, to discriminate between Haitian politicians and its citizens. Haitians are hard workers who start and end each day thankful for all that they have, even if it amounts to the shirt on their back. We are very proud of our country even if we cannot include our government in our pride. The government hasn't supported us; in fact, it has acted to our detriment, guaranteeing that Haiti remains the poorest country in the Western Hemisphere.

Nan tan grangou patat pa gen po
In times of famine, sweet potatoes have no skin
There is virtually no accountability. The

people in command do what they wish, which has resulted in the rich leeching what little Haiti has and, at the same time, inhumane conditions for the rest of us. Our administration does not deem it necessary to prioritize clean water, proper sewage disposal and treatment, or education. Instead they prioritize the size of their own pocketbooks.

Si travay te bon bagay, moun rich la pran-l lontan.
If work were a good thing, the rich would have grabbed it a long time ago.

There have been two upper classes in Haiti: the Grandon, a landowning class, and the Comprador Bourgeoisie, a merchant class. The two classes have battled for power since Haiti's conception, most often using military coups d'état to tip the scales. Each side has ruled with an iron fist, killing thousands of my people only because of a rumor that they disagreed with the political power in place at the time, or for no reason at all. "Disappearances" occurred to the tune of thousands. An ill rumor about a neighbor could in fact result in their death.

Konstitisyon se papie; bayonet se fe.

The constitution is paper; bayonets are steel.

It was during this political climate that I was born. Playing outside was not permitted for the first formative years of my life, partly as a safety precaution and partly because my family was very strict. It was 1986, the year that "Baby Doc," Jean Claude Duvalier, was sent into exile with the help of the United States. Duvalier was the son of "Papa Doc" who was a Medical Doctor, which is how his nickname was coined. Papa Doc declared himself "president for life."

After thousands of human rights violations and embezzlement that is speculated to be in the hundred million range, the United States helped to facilitate his departure. In fact, they picked him up in a cargo plane full of his precious European cars and various other belongings and flew him to his posh exile in France where he remained for years.

13

Baby Doc didn't leave without a fight. Anyone roaming the city was assumed to be a subversive and was punished without evidence. The poorest neighborhoods were raided, and hundreds were massacred simply because of the assumption that the poorest socioeconomic class was involved with the coup.

This too did pass. Once the unrest transformed into greater stability, I was permitted to play outside more frequently, doing what little boys do.

While my childhood has ended, Haiti's political pranks have not. Take this last election for example. The most popular Haitian party was excluded from participating, and the government was not required to provide an explanation.

On voting day the waters became murkier. Millions of citizens were displaced after the earthquake, often many kilometers from their hometown. Many lost their identification cards that were required to vote. I still had mine, but Thaylord did not and was unable to vote. When I arrived at the voting booth I was informed that I was not at the correct location and therefore was not permitted to cast my vote. I asked them where I could cast my vote and I was given a number to call. The voice on the other end of the line informed me that I was many miles from my designated location. They might as well have told me that I was not permitted to vote.

The government declared tap-taps and motorcycles illegal for the duration of the day. There was zero public transportation. If you were rich enough to have your own vehicle then you could drive to your booth; that is, if you were able to discern where exactly that was. Even presidential candidate Jude Célestin arrived at the wrong booth. I watched the event unfold. He was delayed twenty minutes but because of who he was, they permitted him to vote, even as they simultaneously turned me away. After this voting experience the slogan, "Selection, not election" was coined, expressing our frustration and knowledge of the election's fraudulent nature.

Ravet pa janm gen rezon devan poul.

Roaches are never right when facing chickens.

Haitians have learned that we can't depend on or wait for help; instead we must do what is required in order to survive. If we don't like something, the weight is on our shoulders to change it. That is how we became the first free slave state.

I finally understand the gravity of our situation. No one knows what is in store for us in the near future. It's a shame how people can act for power or money.

Housebound

Childhood

My father, Serte Senior, was a quiet, respectable man. Many have told me that our looks are identical, and that he was a good husband. He was blessed with good fortune that landed him a position with Carnival Cruise Lines. With unemployment rates over 70%, this was a miraculous feat. His work kept him out of Haiti for many years.

Each time he returned to Haiti, he and my mother conceived another son. He returned one last time when he was 27; only instead of adding to our family, he contracted and died of pneumonia. I was almost three years old, Thaylord was seventeen months old, and Serte Jr. was four.

When I turned four, job prospects for my mother had dried up, so she set out to a French island, Guadeloupe, securing work as a hospital aide. She left us under the care of our Great Aunt Ovencile, whom we called our Godmother because she was my mom's Godmother. At four years of age, I couldn't understand why she left. Few words were exchanged. However, our connection transcended words and required nothing to sustain it. The change was enormous for someone of my age to experience. I believe that it has made me stronger and more resilient, and has helped prepare me for worse trials that were still ahead.

My Aunt Ovencile and I were already very close. Even before my mom left, my brothers and I spent a great deal of time at her house. She lived a few houses away, and having no kids, cherished

22

our time together.

My mom was often busy so we would play and sleep over at my aunt's house. She was highly respected in the community. Even parents who usually would not allow their children out made an exception if they were headed to her house.

I know very little about my mother's time in Guadeloupe, only that she worked at a hospital and met a French man with whom she conceived my sister. I met Elodie once when she was three; she seemed nice. When mom left, she never said when she would return. We spoke on the phone on occasion. I missed her dearly; however, in her absence I was well looked after. My Aunt Ovencile was very supportive and cared for me as if I were her own child.

I was not a very good kid; I did many things that later earned me a few smacks. She was strict and ruled with a wicked backhand, but I learned many lessons under her care. One lesson in particular was very important to her; I was taught to always offer a greeting. If I was walking down a street with my aunt and did not greet a passerby, I would certainly hear about it when we returned home. I count my blessings for having had her in my life, and I'm certain that she made me a better man than I could have been without her influence.

Scanning through my childhood memories, the clear favorite occurred when I was ten years old. I was shooting hoops with Wilbens at the nearby park when a car slowly approached. My stomach instinctually dropped. My soul understood that this was a special person arriving. I saw a beautiful woman exit the vehicle wearing an enormous grin. I didn't recognize her. It had been over six years since she had left, and I was so young that her face had slowly faded from my memory. Wilbens, in an overwhelmed, trembling voice that I had never heard, exclaimed, "That's our mom!" Still stubborn, I muttered, "Our mom is not in this country." Then my Aunt Ovencile, who had been resting on a nearby bench, chimed in, "That is your mom, and my sister!" She had successfully surprised all of us with an unannounced visit.

Tears flooded down my face, my voice trembling uncontrollably. As an eleven-year-old boy wishing to see his mother, I needed to hug her to prove to myself that she was not a cruel mirage. She held me tightly; I never wanted this moment to end. She whispered, "I am here just for you." I felt like we had a special connection that was just our own. Thaylord was almost two years younger than I was and couldn't remember her like I could. My mom stayed with us for an entire month.

That was by far the best month of my life. We played, sang, shopped, and stargazed together as a family. It was as if time was frozen and there wasn't a care in the world.   Our nirvana abruptly ceased when she returned to Guadeloupe.   Less than two months later she was gone.

I couldn't wrap my mind around the idea that, one second, we were dancing, singing, and hugging, and the next moment she was lifeless. Some friends of the family in Guadeloupe called my aunt to inform us of our loss.   Since Haitians avoid talking about death and accidents, all that Aunt Ovencile would share was that she had a fever and headache; three days later she passed.   She was thirty-three. Initially I refused to believe it. It couldn't be possible; I had seen her with my own eyes.   She looked happy and healthy.   They must be mistaken.

Eventually, with the help of my aunt, I conceded my loss.   She taught me to "turn the page" and dwell not on that which cannot be changed. Experiencing the gamut of intense emotions within three months manifested a degree of angst that I never imagined could be topped.

I don't reference my childhood often, since the sad moments stack high in number.   Instead, I have learned to focus on today and what I have the power to change. Life has so much to offer, and while I did not find the sweet honey while I was young, things got drastically better for me when I went to secondary school.

It felt as if someone had sucker punched me in the stomach, forcefully expelling the air out when I learned that my mom had died. I never knew my father, and had only just reacquainted with my mother. My conceptions regarding the safe haven that parents provided died with them both. As a young boy I needed someone to latch onto. Aunt Ovencile did not disappoint. She understood my grief, taught me about life and how to be a man.

27

Aunt Ovencile was my stand-in mother from age four to eleven. I eventually referred to her as mom. A short year after my mother died, my Aunt Ovencile suffered an acute episode of hypertension that lead to a fatal stroke. With only the month-long visit encompassing my memory of my biological mom, Aunt Ovencile's death was absorbed with greater difficulty. I dealt with my grief quietly for some time.

Shortly thereafter, my mom's older sister, Aunt Miralia, took us under her wing and has continued to care for us to this day. Aunt Miralia is an amazing woman who is known for her tongue. She kept us boys in line by her constant reminders of how we could be better people.

While she didn't utilize the backhand that my great aunt did, her whip of a tongue could be just as, if not more, effective. I recall nights when she stormed into my sleeping area yelling about something I had done wrong many days, and often, weeks prior. I refrained from many activities because it just wasn't worth hearing about them for months to come.

I cannot deny that our childhood suffered great losses; however, I believe that Wilbens and I were very fortunate. We had a family that loved us and took us in as their own sons. We were never abandoned and always cared for. I could have ended up an orphan many times throughout my life. I don't feel regret nor harbor anger towards higher powers because I have everything that I need, and that is much more than many of my Haitian brothers.

Childhood

(The boy above lives in the pictured

median on one of the busiest roads in

Haiti)

28 Seconds

28 Seconds

4:23pm

I was in mid-stride when the earth below revolted in a surprise attack, an angry up-and-down jolt, reverberating with cracking sounds that seemed to originate from every direction. It stunned me, halting me in my tracks. The earth immediately sent a second act of fury, this time with an appallingly deadly side-to-side sweeping motion. In a simultaneous act, almost as if my surroundings had been rigged for a scheduled demolition, structures collapsed sending a blast of air filled with cement, plaster, and other dust particles shooting in every direction, conquering the sun in one disastrous second. Life passed in slow motion. Disaster in a quantity that I could not entertain in my most horrific of dreams was playing out before my eyes, in the dark of day.

4:15pm

I was helping a friend with his physics homework when 28 seconds and one decision forever changed my life.

Drawing class is not my favorite subject. It is required for my engineering degree. It wouldn't be so bad if my teacher weren't so awkwardly goofy. Plus, he didn't impart in me any gems that I feel like I would miss out on if I were to skip his class. So, Tuesday the twelfth, that's exactly what I did. The sun was blazing in its tropical glory. People, cars, trucks, motorcycles and dust darted in every direction. It was a typical day in Port-au-Prince.

4:54pm

Once the eerie cracking from the earth below ceased, screaming commenced, and continued for 48 torturous hours. I yelled toward each structure, "Earthquake, get out!" Looking left, right, and forward through the dimly lit streets I saw

34

bodies strewn everywhere. Then, I realized it was not just bodies; body parts and blood were everywhere.

Later I returned to the school that I was supposed to be attending and saw a pile of rubble. I heard the screams of my classmates crushed inside the flattened structure. I didn't know what to do. I did not have any medical training, but I thought, "I have to help." After the third person that I attempted to help, I came to the realization that there was nothing that I could do for them. Instead, finding my family and home became my priority. A thick particle cloud hung heavy in the sky, blocking the sun's ability to illuminate, creating pitch-black conditions in the middle of the day.

Thankfully, I knew the city well enough to navigate it blindfolded. I sprinted toward my house passing sites that will forever stain my eyes and heart, images that I would not wish on my worst enemy. People were aimlessly roaming, lost, confused, injured, and frightened. Others were like statues, frozen, in shock and denial of the destruction and loss of life around them. Their wide-open eyes stared directly ahead. It was as if they were peering through reality into a different dimension that provided escape from the devastation that they were emotionally unable to process. People ran in every direction, falling in the darkness over the debris, joining the masses of the injured requiring assistance.

I saw countless mothers lying prone and spread-eagle, their faces buried in the rubble, emitting cries from the deepest of their being, spewing from their souls in mourning. Body parts were scattered along each street I raced down, some small and certainly belonging to a child, others large. Streets were tagged in blood; I now think of that scene and the bloodborne diseases that were likely present. On 1-12, however, we were not thinking about pathogens. Instead, concern for humanity, for the lives of our fellow brothers and sisters, consumed our shell-shocked minds.

The police in a nearby station attempted to

help a cluster of blood-ridden hysterics, but had little control over the situation. I wanted to help, but I couldn't stop. I needed to find out if my aunt, brothers, and cousin were still alive, and if I had a home. I was tortured with the uncertainty of my family's wellbeing for my entire run across the city, but each time I saw a victim my focus shifted to the loss. It was incredibly confusing, with my conflicted and wandering mind operating on the worst imaginable type of sensory overload.

After treading through a river and sprinting many kilometers, I closed in on home. I let out a sigh of relief upon seeing that it still stood strong and my weeping family members were alive and incredibly relieved to see that I, too, had survived.

Aunt Miralia charged me, clutching me in a way that seemed as if she would never let go, repeating that she would not lose me again. For the moments that I was gone, she had been certain that I had perished along with my classmates.

Wilbens had yet to arrive home. My aunt was frantic. I kept telling her, "Everything will be ok. He is fine, we will all be ok." But I had no proof of what I was saying. I was scared, but I tried very hard to remain calm and not show any of my fear because it would only make matters worse.

Wilbens arrived three hours later; we had all survived. Few Haitian families fared the same. In spite of my aunt's protests, Wilbens and I set out to check on our friends. We departed in a sprint throughout the particle-ridden, dimly lit city.

4:23pm

I had just left school, concerned that I may not be re-admitted next year because of my academic probation status. Then a huge bulldozer slammed its wrecking ball into a structure adjacent to me; at least that is what I thought at first. I had never felt an earthquake before. I immediately sat down in the street not knowing what else I should do. The gyrating continued. Then I heard people screaming; I saw blood and collapsed houses. I immediately wanted to forget these sights but knew that I wouldn't be able to rid my memory of such a horrific scene.

Running through the streets with Thaylord after the disaster was comparable to nothing. Death and destruction was in front, behind, to each side, below and above us. It consumed our senses. The smell was a combination of cement, dust, dirt, blood, sweat, and later rotting flesh. My eyes burned and struggled, working overtime, due to the ominous black cloud that obstructed the sun.

I saw the true humanity that connects us - pain, torment, relief, death, injury, illness, and everything in between. There were those who were praising the Lord above with song and prayer, giving thanks that they survived and others cursing the same God for taking their loved ones. I heard cement cracking indicating its continued battle with gravity. Cries filled the air: cries of trapped victims scared and in acute physical pain, and cries from mourning families.

I felt the thick layer of dust coating my body. The sun's absence caused a slight drop in temperature, yet I was drenched in sweat. My heart beat rapidly; sleep was a stranger to me. All my senses were heightened, my coordination swift, my night vision keen from the adrenalin that flooded my body. I felt debris under my feet with each stride. Thaylord and I were extra cautious with our footwork to avoid falling or stepping on any bodies.

Wilbens and I arrived at my school to find that my classmates did in fact perish. The nursing school was adjacent to my engineering school. My best friend had been attending class along with 700

other students when the earthquake hit. Youselande and I had grown up together. We met while attending boarding school and had remained close friends ever since. She simply disappeared; I never saw her or any of the other 700 nursing students again.

In addition to my personal loss, our country's loss flooded my mind. What a difficult and ironic time to lose all of the country's aspiring nurses. Little remained; the pile of rubble had comprised the majority of Haitian college structures. Haiti's two major colleges, one private and one public, both suffered damage.

I located Georgeton, a buddy of mine who said that when the quake hit he was with one of his close friends. Georgeton sprawled prone in the middle of the street, but his friend ran towards a building. Georgeton yelled, unsuccessfully, "Come back, it's not safe!" His friend entered the structure and seconds later was killed by its collapse. He witnessed the entire event while lying helplessly prone in the street. While he recounted the nightmare to me, his eyes appeared vacant and misty, clearly still in a daze.

The sky was still a memory; I was well aware that it was there but was unable to locate it. Instead, my sense of smell exposed that time was indeed passing. Time directly related to the intensity of the stench of the rotting human remains.

The smell was the needed smack in the face to those who were still stunned, forcing them back into reality and to the realization that their basic needs were not being met. People flooded the streets, begging for food, water, and clothing. The little that they once possessed been obliterated by thousands of pounds of cement.

In the Days Following 1/12

The next morning tested the theory of Survival of the Fittest. People looted any store that they could gain entry to, gathering food or common goods. In an attempt to maintain order, police shot looters on sight. The desperation of the people outweighed the concern of being shot tenfold. Looters were not deterred; the only result was an increase in corpses and loss.

The city became a cemetery. Corpses lined each street, seeming to multiply as more bodies were removed from the collapsed structures. The government did nothing to help us; they fled and watched us suffer on TV.

The international head came to our aid by assisting in body removal. We were told to place the bodies in the street, and they would be picked up. It took an entire week to remove the bodies. For seven days we had to bear the stench of the disease-ridden corpses.

For seven days, we were forced to walk past or over bodies lining our largest city. Wilbens and I coated our noses with toothpaste so that we could bear the odor. Anyone who located a facemask wore it so as to inhale fewer particles from the cloud that consumed the city.

It was impossible to identify bodies and

administer the appropriate death ceremonies due to the great health concern that the deceased posed. Instead, the bodies were discarded by any means possible. Records were not maintained. Bodies were carted away in grocery carts and wheelbarrows. Tractors lifted piles of corpses into dump and trash trucks. Some bodies were even burned in piles in impromptu cremations. Those that were hauled out of Port-au-Prince were dumped in mass graves, some into the same graves that housed Haiti's enemies, a huge taboo for our cultural beliefs of death and the afterlife. I was never afforded closure for loss of the people whom I loved. No goodbyes were spoken. Our loved ones simply vanished.

Two desperate days passed before I saw any aid arrive. During that time it was difficult not knowing if, or when, help would arrive. Without access to water or food, I saw many people who would die without intervention. It was a glimpse into what losing an entire nation would look like. I hope that we will remember these circumstances, so that we can incite the people to change our dependent system.

Luckily, my family had a small supply of water and food that sustained us until aid was available. Since we didn't know when we would have access to more food, we stretched out our supply as much as possible. The stress of the horrific environment helped me to stave off hunger.

The Dominican Republic was the first to arrive to our aid approximately two days after the earthquake. They brought with them much needed water and energy bars. I can't say for sure when they arrived because days and nights blended for me. I was not the only one with sleepless nights.

People strutted the streets all hours of the night. Many of those who had housing preferred to attempt to sleep in the streets, even amongst the deceased, for fear that another earthquake would kill them if they remained in a structure. Many citizens attributed their survival to the fact that they were outside when the earthquake struck. It was months before people felt safe enough to enter structures; even mass was held outside.

It seemed like an eternity before other countries arrived to provide assistance. In actuality, it was probably about three or four days. The United States took over our airport with a sea of green tents, hummers, and cargo planes. I heard that they wouldn't allow Doctors Without Borders to land their plane, which was loaded with a desperately needed inflatable hospital, detouring them twice to the Dominican Republic. I know that the US had a job to do, but I think that we needed the hospital more than we needed the hummers.

The United Nations had an influx of personnel patrolling in jeeps, automatic weapons strung across their chest, suited in full battle gear as if they were preparing for war. Slowly, non-governmental agencies (NGOs) flooded our streets with magnet designators displayed on their new vehicles: Doctors without Borders, American Red Cross, Heart to Heart International. The list went on and on.

I will never forget that day... I lost part of me...

Teeth Not Tears

Identity Crisis

Identity Crisis

Jean Fournes Thaylord will always be Haitian. No matter where I live or what I do for work, the blood that pumps through my heart is Haitian. Sadly, as time plays out, the expression of our culture, what exactly it means to be Haitian, has become murky along with our water. Years ago, we practiced traditions that were handed down to us from our ancestors in Western Africa, and the indigenous populations who inhabited Hispaniola before Christopher Columbus arrived. Our culture was rich, and we provided for ourselves with the fruits of our labor.

My great grandparents worshiped African gods and our ancestors' spirits without criticism. Our beliefs, behaviors, and science were based on timeless traditions that spanned as far back as the genealogy line records. Much of our beliefs and practices today are derived from modern science and societal expectations. Drastic changes occurred during the nineteen years that the United States occupied Haiti. My family has always lamented how, ever since then, things have never been the same.

The residual societal dream erodes our rich history as my fellow citizens attempt to live like anyone else, especially Americans. Only, we are not Americans; we are Haitians motivated by the incompatible values of a developed nation.

Trade has allowed the international community to dominate what would potentially be our commerce. Our clothes and food are from the States. We eat less local food every day due to heavily subsidized imported foods. It confuses me that foods that are picked and shipped across the Caribbean Sea cost less than the produce grown here in our soil. The average Haitian agricultural family of six brings in five hundred dollars or less annually. It's no shock that rice and beans is our national dish. Fewer people can turn a profit with the work of our hands, since our country is void of natural resources and now fewer educational institutions. We are moving in a dangerous direction. A friend recently regretted, "First the earthquake, then cholera, then the disaster..."

As a Christian, I am an excellent example of the change that resulted from the US occupation. Once Haiti regained power, over 80 percent of Haitians self-identified as Catholic and/or Christian. A common saying in Haiti is that "Haitians are 70 percent Catholic, 30 percent Protestant, and 100 percent Voodou." This explains how many of my Catholic friends practice Voodou side by side with Catholicism. My family frowns on this because of what the missionaries and priests told them. I'm not sure if I agree with my family. To me, the two religions are the same except for the names of the gods we worship. Our African gods are just like the Catholic saints and are worshiped in a similar way.

Both religions believe and worship God. The missionary movement, both today and during the US occupation, tries relentlessly to rid Voodou and other cultural practices that they don't see fit to co-exist with their conception of a Catholic Haiti.

I didn't learn much about Voodou until I was an adult and taught Social Studies. Thaylord and I never practiced Voodou, but I have learned about the history of the tradition.

I would like to learn more since it is part of my culture, which I treasure. What I do know is that over a million slaves were "imported" to Haiti in the late 1700's. Their white masters forced them to practice Catholicism.

Naturally, my ancestors did not want to be told how to express their spirituality, but they also practiced self-preservation. In order to please their masters and remain in control of their spirituality, they praised Catholic icons like Mary, John, James, and Peter; only they carried over the names and attributes of their African gods for each of the Catholic icons. When the master saw them praying, he was satisfied, not realizing that they were seeking counsel from their African gods. Even now, many Haitians practice Voodou, and self-identify as Catholic.

Voodou and Catholic rituals share similarities due to Voodou's origins. Voodou ceremonies are conducted throughout the countryside but are rare in the city. Practitioners seek help through ceremonies created around a specific god, whose icon is celebrated and worshiped throughout the ceremony. Voodou priests, viewed much like prophets, bless the ceremony and use spiritual gifts to discover and restore problems in their constituents. Music, especially the Racime genre, plays an important role in the ceremonies.

I also learned a lot of what I know about Voodou while working at a factory that sold Voodou icons to tourists as a cultural memento. I learned about Ergelie, whose Catholic equivalent is Mary. Her icon is identical to Mary, but Ergelie is a member of the Loa, an African god from whom we seek help. The Loa are often called upon for protection, especially during hurricane season. I learned about many of the gods and their powers. Not one of them was malicious in nature. They were uplifting spirits.

The dolls are used to focus prayer and worship. They are no different than Catholic statues, rosary beads, or a cross necklace for that matter.

56

The famous pins used in conjunction with Voodou dolls are rarely used. When they are used, their purpose is to focus attention on one portion of the body or soul, usually to enact healing energy to that location. Like anything shared by the masses, there are those who interpret and use the power in a negative light, but that is not the true nature of Haitian Voodou.

Out of respect for my parents, I avoided Voodou ceremonies. One night, however, my curiosity got the better part of me. I peeked into an open door to catch a glimpse of a celebration. I vividly remember the candlelit room, light majestically dancing across the room in tune with the beat of the drum that resonated with every nearby soul. Worshipers danced alongside the candlelight creating a symphony of rhythmic movement whose crescendo mirrored the unique percussion.

I've been told that Voodou ceremonies vary greatly, depending on the occasion that is being celebrated. Sometimes, the ancestors appear in spirit and embody a member. The possessed member then acts out the spirit's wishes, which may include healing family members or offering direction for an individual. As the spirit leaves the body, I have been told that violent shaking occurs as the exorcism manifests.

No matter what the choice method for worshipping is, it is needed. Haiti is going from bad to worse. Most of us are uneducated. Fifty percent of the population has access to schools, that is, before the earthquake destroyed them, and less than ten percent complete higher education. Jobs are scarce, and the best candidate is usually not selected. It is who you know that gets you work. My Haitian education places me behind candidates that received their education abroad. That seems backwards to me.

Cultivation

Cultivation

God provided a miracle for Wilbens and me with our admission to a tuition-free Catholic secondary school. Louverture Cleary was a boarding school for underprivileged kids of Haiti, sponsored by a church in Rhode Island. Before boarding school I was reserved, my spirit somber, full of confusion about my past experiences. I recall walking into the school at twelve years of age understanding that I was to live here for the next seven years. What I did not know was that I would never be the same.

The staff's hospitality was second to none, easing my transition and steep learning curve. I had not been exposed to much diversity prior to school. My classmates had an array of backgrounds, beliefs, and political views. I learned to appreciate the differences that comprise our individuality when making friends for the first time. I learned to smile my way through life, thankful for all that I had been given and thankful for all of the opportunities that I have yet to experience.   My ambitions grew, and my fears dissipated.

When my aunt told me that we were going to the Catholic school I was scared. I fought it at first. My older brother, Serte Junior, was attending the government school and I wanted to go with him. I didn't know anyone at the boarding school and was scared to be away from home for so long. My aunt knew of my desire to learn English. Once she told me that I would learn English at the Catholic school I gave up my fight and told her that I would attend.

The new routine was difficult to adjust to. I didn't have the habit to wake up early. Our day began at 5:30 in the morning for first meeting, then breakfast; school started at 7:30am. We had classes until 4:30pm with a five-minute break every hour and a thirty-minute lunch.

After about six months, I fell in love with the school and did not want to leave when I graduated. Secondary schools in Haiti are seven years in length; in that time I made friendships that I will embrace for a lifetime.

It was forbidden to have a relationship in the school, and it would have been difficult to sneak because we had unisex residences. Needless to say, I didn't have a girlfriend, but I did have a crush on one girl that I was too scared to pursue. Instead, I nurtured close platonic relationships. I made best friends with Valery and Oscar and had a group of seven people who I spent all of my time with. We were a family and shared all that we had with one another.

I had a few relationships, but it was a huge secret, a logistical nightmare. If the administration had found out I would have been placed on probation, or worse, expelled. The rules were strict because the laws in Haiti mandated it. If my school had one publicly known pregnancy they could be shut down by Haitian authorities. My guardian and I were required to sign an agreement stating that I would not partake in a relationship with anyone during my seven-year stay in school. Thankfully, I was never caught.

At twelve years old, I had no fear entering the school that I would live and learn in Sunday through Friday. I had never been away from my family before, but my fears were kept at bay with constant reassurances issued by Wilbens. He couldn't say enough positive things about his experiences there. He told me that I would have to work hard but that it would be an amazing time. He was right; my teachers were very supportive. They knew that it was hard to live far from my parents.

In actuality, we were only ten miles away but on Haitian roads that translated to a two-hour drive. The school created an environment where I sometimes forgot that I was far from home because the school simulated a family. We laughed, played, studied, and ate together. I learned that I loved science and chemistry, which continue to be my favorite subjects.

My insomnia started when I was a junior in high school. One of my good friends and classmate was shot and killed on his way home from school. We were roommates in 2005 and played basketball together frequently. His family lived in the worst slum in Port-au-Prince, Cité Soleil. I have battled insomnia ever since.

67

The school assigned roommates based on last names, so Thaylord and I were bunkmates. We attended school, played soccer and basketball, did our chores, ate, and studied together. We grew closer than ever before and still consider each other best friends. Meanwhile, Serte Jr. attended the government school. He worked with a local NGO when he wasn't attending classes at the University. Only visiting with him on occasional Saturdays, we slowly drifted apart. We were both studying economics, but the age difference and geographic difference were hard to overcome. He couldn't compete with our inside jokes, stories and deep understanding of one another.

Graduation was riddled with mixed feelings. I was so happy to have been successful, receiving passing scores for all of my classes. I made my family and my family away from home, the staff at Louverture Clearly, proud. Deep down, I was terrified. I didn't want to leave. This was my home. I had grown into the man that I now am while living there. It was my safe haven, my sanctuary. Nothing bad could reach me there. Regardless of how I felt, it was time to continue my journey.

Valery, my best friend helped land me a job with the factory that made Voodou dolls, purses, and other cultural crafts. I saved all of my money so that I could attend college, but it was not enough. I applied for every scholarship that I qualified for, but in the end was unsuccessful. Valery's outcome was better. He received a full scholarship to the public university in his desired subject, International Studies. I wanted to study the same discipline but it was dreadfully expensive. Ironically, the only subject that I could afford to study was Economics...

I studied hard, but it didn't come naturally to me. Also, my work at the factory was not agreeable to my exam schedule. I saved up my vacation days so that I could use them when scheduling conflicted with exams. However, when I used my vacation day, my employer often called me into work the morning I was scheduled off. As a result, I was placed on academic probation.

After I graduated secondary school I placed in the University of Haiti as an Engineering student. It was a huge feat; I learned that I scored 7th out of 32,324 candidates on basic testing in math, science, French, and chemistry. They only had 50 spots, so I was elated to learn that I made it! My focus is on solar energy. If I wasn't studying, I was playing soccer. I was a mid-fielder for UH. Playing soccer was a great de-stressor. I lost myself while I played, focusing my thoughts on strategy and movement. It was a much-needed break from constant academia. I was doing fairly well in school.

After the earthquake destroyed my college I took that energy and used it to work six days a week for Heart to Heart International as a translator for their medical clinic. All the while, I did not know if or when I would be able to complete my studies. I worked with other Haitian college students who were in the same situation; one was a third year student in medical school. It was a tough predicament, but it was ours and we were not going to let it keep us down. I knew that we would be better people because of it.

Every ten days a new set of Heart to Heart volunteers arrived in Haiti. It was an amazing experience. Without the earthquake I never would have met all of these wonderful people. I now have friends from around the globe. People came and showed me love by spending their time and money here to help those who they did not know.

It was a bit difficult to tell my story regarding the quake over and over, reliving my nightmare for the curious minds. I figure that it was the least that I could do for the volunteers who did so much for my country.

Peyi ONG

The Republic of NGOs

Teeth Not Tears

Even before the earthquake, Haiti hosted more NGOs than any other country. We are often referred to as "The Republic of NGOs". Their productivity and work vary so greatly that I can't make any all-inclusive statements. The Red Cross and UNICEF are two that I am constantly impressed with. I've watched them work, drenched in sweat, around the clock, battling Cholera, while simultaneously building treatment facilities for us. On the opposite end of the spectrum are other agencies that do very little, or we have no clue what they are doing.

I've heard complaints that the influx of NGOs is responsible for our gas shortages and horribly clogged roads. People who make these claims are the minority, and I don't agree with their view. Those who have come here to help are a gift from above, and I am eternally grateful. The fact that so many volunteers have chosen to come here and use their money to help me and my brothers and sisters whom they have never met is heroic and will never be forgotten.

Some argue that after a year of work, more progress could have been made. I argue that we as Haitians need to claim responsibility for progress, creating change ourselves. If our government had been doing what is necessary to run a country, then we wouldn't be dependent on external agencies to meet our basic needs. As that is not the case, I believe that many more of us would have died without international intervention.

There are numerous questions addressing how to proceed with relief and the reconstruction of Haiti. One that I am frequently asked is whether relief money should funnel through the government. I say, heck no! Things would be even worse than they are now! Our government is corrupt; no one would know where the money would go. Giving the money to the government is as good as burning it. Our government's inability to govern has been demonstrated through its relationship with the NGOs. One would think it simplistic to coordinate and oversee the NGOs providing relief. Doing so would guarantee a national cooperation of rebuilding efforts. Instead, my government continues to prove its incompetency to govern by failing to maintain even a basic record of entities providing relief work in the country, a simple role call. If they cannot manage a few thousand NGOs, how are they supposed to govern 9 million people?

If I were the deciding body, I would keep the money out of the government's sticky hands. I would also require NGO communication through the government so that efforts could be coordinated and Haitian administration would participate in the country's reconstruction.

Peyi ONG

My brother and I disagree about NGOs but agree that we bear the ultimate responsibility for our country's successes and failures. I have always believed that NGOs are here primarily for a piece of the pie, a $10.5 billion dollar pie. I don't think that they are much different from our own government.

In poor countries like this one, we are satisfied with food and water. The mass majority doesn't think about tomorrow, as their stomach is full today. This formula leads to exploitation, and the NGOs capitalize on it. They are primarily interested in making money. If some assistance is rendered, then that is a bonus and something that they can capture, bring home, and display while they make more money.

NGOs give us fish to feed us for a day, but they do not teach us to fish and thereby feed us for a lifetime. That is not to say that some of the people who are involved with the agencies don't have good intentions. I look at the NGOs collectively. I believe good intentions are weaved in and out of NGOs, but their guts, the driving force are those of a business that is determined to make money and gain popularity. Notoriety equals fiscal power.

I'm sure some organizations do better jobs than others, but I have the same general impression about them all. Sure, the Red Cross has been helpful, but I don't think that UNICEF is very productive. They are supposed to help children and here in Haiti, children are mistreated, malnourished, have slim to no educational opportunities an entire year after the earthquake. I recognize that UNICEF is not responsible for any of these injustices, but I will not give them accolades for their work if I cannot see the fruits of it.

The Republic of NGOs

Bondye fe san di; Neg di san fe.

God acts and doesn't talk;

People talk and don't act.

I agree with Thaylord that they cannot be blamed for the fuel shortages and increased congestion because, as Haitians, it is our responsibility to solve these shortfalls. However, I do believe that they play a role in contributing to the problem. I don't understand why so many agencies insist on acquiring brand new gas-guzzling SUVs. If their true purpose were to help us, then why would they spend so much of their donated funds on new automobiles?

If I had to choose an organization that I thought was doing a good job, I would choose Handicap International because it lightens the burden for our handicapped people. I've seen them restore hope and usefulness to many of our disabled.

Cholera

A Bacterial Aftershock

Cholera: A Bacterial Aftershock

Surviving the earthquake has been an indescribable feat. It has cultivated strength from the depths of my soul to a capacity previously unimaginable so that I am able to get up every day and forge on. Then came Cholera...

I couldn't help but think, "Haven't we seen enough death?" Again we are tallying up our lost ones; only this aftershock has no foreseeable end. In just five months we have seen over 231,000 cases and roughly 4,500 deaths.

The strand of Cholera that struck our already critically injured country was consistent with a strand found in regions of Asia where UN workers have recently been stationed. Haiti has harbored ideal conditions for Cholera bacteria but did not have a single case prior to the UN occupation.

The epidemic is suspected to have resulted from inappropriate human waste disposal into our great river. This same river provides water for us to bathe, drink and wash our clothes. Numerous people died in the first weeks that Cholera struck Haiti. They presented with vomiting and acute diarrhea but had no idea what caused it nor sought out medical attention. Many died the day after onset of symptoms.

Once the culprit was identified, surprisingly, the government worked tirelessly to cease its progress. Unfortunately, the bacteria reached every area of our country. So far, thank the Lord, I have not lost anyone close to me to Cholera. Only God can do something for us in this situation; there is nothing that we can do but try to get each meal and share with one another.

Bondye do ou: fe pa ou; M a fe pa M.

God says: do your part; and I'll do mine.

Cholera is a torturous disease. People have died throughout the country, in the city and in the rural areas alike. The deaths are slow and painful. Cholera makes its way inside of your belly through infected water or food then wreaks havoc. It changes your cells in a way that causes them to dump all of their fluid into the intestines. The stark dehydration, when left untreated, is quickly lethal.

Cholera: A Bacterial Aftershock

The worst thing about it is the way people have dealt with it. Cholera is natural, but human sewage in our water source is not. The government should protect our water, and assure that these violations do not occur. It has been half a year since the inception of Cholera, and what has our government learned? Nothing. They have not modified, changed, or improved our waste disposal or fresh water systems in any way. Still today, there are people disposing of sewage in our water.

I don't like to say that the UN is responsible for the outbreak or spread of Cholera; I don't see it that way. We all are responsible for what happened. Nothing can replace the lives lost. The question is, how can we solve the problem? We need access to clean water. We are on a tropical island, for crying out loud, how do we not have access to water? If we go on with our status quo, in 10-20 years we are likely to contract a disease far worse than Cholera.

Cholera Bacteria

Many are upset that our government has not condemned the MINUSTAH (French acronym for the UN's mission in Haiti) for bringing this bacterial aftershock to us so recklessly. Instead, the authorities keep their politically correct mouths shut, just as they are instructed to do so from the big guns: France and the United States.

The Haitian government is not performing an

investigation; instead MINUSTAH is going to investigate internally. What exactly is that supposed to prove? "I checked with myself and all looks good..." Because President Préval is trying to appease those abroad, his own populace has revolted. When reports arrived that MINUSTAH was responsible for the Cholera outbreak, there were huge demonstrations. Thousands of people went to the UN site and chanted for their removal.

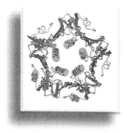

For the first few months, Cholera was on everyone's mind. It was what everyone talked about it; who did they know was infected, how were they going to avoid it, and so on. People had an aversion to touch, for fear of spreading germs.

Five months later, the Hatian Cholera

endemic plateaued. Numbers of the infected descended for the first time since Cholera's inception. Thousands of people fight the war against Cholera, cognizant that if they stop, it is likely that a huge comeback would result. When one person in the home contracts it, everyone else residing there will soon follow. I am concerned about contracting the disease but my knowledge regarding prevention and signs and symptoms, along with my faith, award me security.

Even though the UN undoubtedly carried the beast into our country, I believe that ultimate responsibility lies with our government. Authorities should require clean physicals of those who wish to live and work in Haiti, whether civilian or military. More diligence should be used before permitting thousands of people to enter our country. Especially since Nepal had an outbreak of Cholera, a screening should have been mandatory for any individual transferring from Nepal to Haiti. Haitian authorities should also mandate waste removal procedures for MINUSTAH and any other agency that we are hosting. I recognize that my vantage is narrow and my governing experience nill; however, I believe that a little common sense and regulation could have thwarted this beast.

There was talk about a vaccine that could prevent Cholera. I am not sure why it never arrived. I heard from my American friend that it came down to logistics and money. Regardless, if there was a cure and people withheld it to a starving, dying community, that is not right. I like to assume the best in people and choose to believe that it was not sent because we are getting better without it.

New Haiti

Many countries are deciding what the "New Haiti" should be like. I understand that they have a fiscal interest, but why do they believe that this gives them the right to decide how our country should be reconstructed? The United States wants us to become an industrial country so that we can host many factories providing them cheap labor.

Our government needs to take a leadership role, and organize what is best for us, complete with blue prints, and a theme for our New Haiti, if one is ever to be built. Who knows what we need better than we do? I, however, don't believe in the reconstruction of Haiti. I believe that the NGOs the government will eat up all of the money. Having that been said, if I were given a paintbrush and

93

Haiti as my canvas, I would create a Haiti that was as beautiful as the Dominican Republic. The beauty that the DR boasts has been said to surpass that of Miami's. I've never been to Miami, but it sounds pretty spectacular. I would plant thousands of trees, to correct our deforestation. Roads that traversed the country would be constructed with the understanding that if we rebuild Port-au-Prince and do not expand into the rest of the country, then we will have worked without advancement.

We need to spread out and diversify our economy. I would accomplish this by building at least two ports, and a handful of cities so that numerous jobs would be created and our citizens can all have space to live. It is necessary to spread out the nine million residents of Port-au-Prince. Those nine million currently live in less than fourteen square miles. This would result in a decrease in unemployment. Currently we are 90% unemployed. Also, if we were to experience another natural disaster, the loss of life would be reduced since we would be less concentrated.

I would reignite our agricultural community. We need to grow, harvest, and consume our own food again. I would put in place a conditional reward system for those who maintain crops, giving them free land provided they produce food. The livelihoods of those who grow crops are threatened when we allow heavily subsidized foods into our country. Imported foods should not cost less than local foods. One day our free food handouts will end. Then what will we eat?

Our administration needs to capitalize on our popularity in the news. Up to this point, the NGOs have done a much better job making money on our famed poverty. We need to capitalize on this and bring in tourists, make Port-au-Prince a memorial site, much like Ground Zero, or Pearl Harbor; only our site resulted from an act of God. We need to design how people remember us, rather than allowing other groups to decide that for us.

I would restrict what services were permitted

to exist in Haiti, utilizing temporary permits that were eligible for renewal so that we can keep tabs on who is here, what they are doing, and if their products are what we wish to have continued. The "Republic of NGOs" is impeding our possible launch of a new economy. We cannot compete with free.

I am clearly no politician, but what I would like to do for work is teach computer engineering to my Haitian brothers and sisters. Many Haitians don't even know about the Internet, how to use a computer, or even how to type. I believe that if they understood the concept of the World Wide Web, then they could augment creative thinking and generate a living through international business. It could be our key to exit poverty.

That is my goal, to help educate people. Many Haitians who were fortunate enough to make it to the university didn't even have an email address. If we want to grow up and have a better life, there are some things that we should know about.

How simple it is to see that all the worry in the world cannot control the future. We can only be happy now, and there will never be a time that is not now.

Wow, a lot needs to be done. Looking at it all at once is a bit overwhelming. I believe everything starts with a good education. A good education is required for a strong nation. The long-term solution is to teach our children to become creative problem solvers. This education would lead us to know how and where to rebuild.

New Haiti

Piti, piti, wazo fe nich li.

Little by little, the bird builds its nest.

Personally, I hope to help rebuild Haiti as an electrical engineer. I want to take the education that I have been given and continue to pay it back to Haiti. I do not see myself as one who could teach other Haitians because I just don't have the patience or see myself doing a good job. But I am not trained to know how to rebuild a nation. I simply believe in education and its power to provide.

Teeth Not Tears

The Strength "Pwisans" of Haiti

PWISANS

I am no different than you. In fact, if given the same circumstances, I am sure that you would do the same, if not better, than I have done. The human spirit is stronger than I had ever dreamt. While I would not wish our suffering on any soul, it has opened my eyes to the range of circumstances that we are capable of enduring. I have met hundreds of lovely people whose lives I would never have had the pleasure to be part of without the devastation of January 12th.

I have no regrets. Yes, I had more than my fill of sorrow growing up and recently, but each trial has made me who I am today. I do not ask for forgiveness or harbor regrets for who I am or what I have experienced. I thank God every day for yet another miracle: each sun up and sun down. I don't complain; instead I do my part to become educated, and apply my skills to enrich Haiti.

Bondye Bon.
God is good.

"Haiti" literally translates to "Land of Mountains" in our indigenous tongue Taíno. My favorite saying in Haitian Creole is, "Deye mon gen mon" which translates to, "Beyond mountains, there are mountains." It is a great illustration of the mystery of life.

We accomplished the ascension of the first large peak on January 1st, 1804 signifying our freedom from slavery. It was a long and treacherous journey from which many people heroically perished. We've seen many smaller mountains since then, some in the form of hurricanes, illness, famine, and corruption.

Possibly, the largest mountain yet was formed on January 12th, 2010. We are still not far from basecamp but are climbing more each day. We are determined to see the fruits of our work from the highest point that Haiti will have seen.

Sonje lapli ki leve maji ou.
Remember the rain that made your corn grow.

Haiti is a country full of smiles because we are resilient, hardworking, and positive people. We are patient, and know that in the end this indeed will pass. If I were sad and wallowed in each negatively perceived event, I would never grow and miss all of the sweetness of life. Life is only lived in the now.

Instead, I see the positive light in each situation. Each day is perfect just as it was created. This is why I smile so much; I have no regrets, no anger, and no fear. Hearing my friends from various countries speak of their troubles, I am led to believe that the less one has, the less they have to fear losing.

PWISANS

The potential that we have as a country was displayed when we became the first free African country. We united hands with a common purpose and stood our ground as brothers and sisters. We displayed the strength that is undeniably Haitian. Unfortunately, I do not see this happening today. While we are no longer slaves, our freedom has been offered up to those who provide us with our basic needs. We now live dependent on outsiders for our next meals, tents, and so on. How can we call ourselves a sovereign state when over 70% of our country's budget comes from the international community? If we linked hands once again for a common purpose, I believe that we could move forward from the tent camps and become a strong nation once again. A year and a half is too long for tents.

Our present actions do not accurately portray our strength as a people. We must come together and say no to the tents, no to international food, and yes to education. Education is the only way out of the hole that we have crawled into. If we were a formally educated people, we would be one step closer to regaining our dignity.

Personally, the largest motivation for me to continue the daily fight is to please my aunt. She has been an angel for me. She raised me, and provided me with a coveted education. It is now my turn to please her by showing her that her efforts were not in vain. I want to give her back what she has given to me, and make her proud. It's my turn.

The variables that weigh in against our recovery are numerous, but I am not concerned. Haiti's strength as a community is gaining momentum; our hearts ache for those who we have lost. At the same time, we are fueled with their spirits and will make them proud, not allowing their death to be in vain. Pain does not stunt our growth; instead it is enzymatic, accelerating change.

We are strong; we know that we will succeed, and we will be smiling.

" As a survivor, I understand that I have a

responsibility to do more than just survive."

5 Months After the Earthquake:

316,000 killed in the earthquake

300,000 injured in the earthquake

1.5 million people displaced

280,000 structures collapsed or severely damaged

Statistics provided by the Haitian government

4,600 killed by cholera

250,000 contracted cholera

US researchers predict 800,000 will be infected by cholera

Less than 5% of rubble has been removed

Less than 10% of the pledged $9 billion has been delivered

More than one million people remain homeless

Statistics provided by the World Health Organization

Afterward: An Update

Jean Fournes Thaylord was blessed with yet another miracle. He met and befriended an extraordinary woman, Karen Chung, who, in her determination to help, formed a sponsorship that enabled him to receive a student visa to study in New Jersey at a community college. He hopes to transfer to a local four-year university after completing his Associates Degree. He lives with a family who has graciously provided housing and meals.

Fundraising efforts have been initiated for his tuition, books, and other expenses. By purchasing this book you have already helped with his education, and I thank you so much. Once his schooling is paid for, we will begin fundraising to bring his brother Wilbens to the United States in order to complete his education. Both Thaylord and Wilbens maintain strong convictions about education and returning to Haiti to bring their newly honed skills to strengthen their community.

If you feel drawn to help financially, you can sponsor them at www.TeethNotTears.com. One hundred percent of the donations reach the Thaylord brothers.

Thaylord is one step closer to his goal of becoming an electrical engineer with an emphasis in solar power.

Wilbens continues to live in Haiti. He recently resigned from his job at the factory because its proximity to Cité Soleil has become too dangerous to justify the risks. He currently volunteers as an interpreter for Heart to Heart International whenever invited.

Wilbens aspires to one day continue his higher education so that he may equip his fellow Haitians with his specialized skills. His educational goals include earning a Bachelor's degree in Computer Engineering, enabling him to teach Computer Science courses in Haiti so that he can bring the world, and all of the potential it holds, to Haiti.

An Excerpt from Karen Chung

When I arrived to Haiti for my one month medical volunteer mission with Heart to Heart, I knew that I would be challenged. Though I was not new to third world countries, what I saw during transit to my accommodation left me stunned. The scale of the destruction in an already impoverished country defied belief.

Amidst the earthquake rubble was a people filled with hope and gleaming Haitian smiles - one of the brightest in particular was that of Jean Fournes Thaylord. Unfortunately, I did not have the opportunity to meet his brothers.

Thaylord's energetic and light-hearted presence persisted in a time of despair and anguish. His dynamic and engaging personality focused on the positive. He threw himself into his job as a translator and befriended each NGO volunteer he encountered.

My last afternoon in Haiti, I decided to treat the translators to a beer. After I made the purchase, I embarrassingly realized that I did not have enough Haitian currency with me to follow through with payment. Without hesitation, Thaylord stepped in, satisfied the remainder of the bill and asked in exchange that I promise to return one day to Haiti. It was hard to understand how he was so eager to give after all that he had lost. This display of generosity and kindness motivated me to find direct ways to help Haiti and its people.

Thaylord has made it to the USA on a student visa that I helped him secure. He is diligently studying to be an electrical engineer with a focus in solar energy so he can bring light to all his countrymen - a noble and productive cause. The unrelenting, focused determination and enthusiasm he brings to his studies and to his life continue to inspire. I am grateful, honored and privileged to know Thaylord. Without a doubt, he embodies the potential for a better Haiti.

Want To Volunteer?

Heart to Heart International is accepting medical volunteers to staff their clinics. -
www.hearttoheart.org
401 S. Clairborne Rd., Suite 302
Olathe, KS 66062
913.764.5200

The University of Miami accepts medical students and licensed professionals to staff their tent hospital. -
http://www.med.miami.edu/haiti-relief
305.243.6501

Glory House Services is uniting the Haitian Community through ESL classes as well as Creole classes that are free of charge in the Kansas City area. -
http://www.gloryhousekc.org
3841 S. Vassar Street
Independence, MO 64052
816.237.0447

Author: Shannon Enete holding a patient while providing care in Haiti as a medical volunteer.

Afterward

Teeth Not Tears

Teeth Not Tears

Afterward

Teeth Not Tears

EDITOR: LEIGH RYSKO

PHOTOGRAPHER: SHANNON ENETE

OTHER EDITS: KAYDEN HOWARD

COVER ARTWORK & FORMATTING: DEIDRE HOF

Made in the USA
Middletown, DE
18 September 2020